THE LIBRARY OF THE PLANETS™

Mars

Amy Margaret

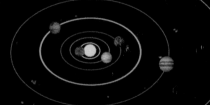

The Rosen Publishing Group's
PowerKids Press™
New York

For Jacob, Daniel, and little Katherine

Published in 2001 by The Rosen Publishing Group, Inc.
29 East 21st Street, New York, NY 10010

First Edition

Book Design: Michael Caroleo and Michael de Guzman

Photo Credits: pp. 1, 4-5, 7 (background), 8 (solar flare background), 11 (planets and Earth's surface) Photodisc; p. 7 © Michael Whelan/NGS Image Collection; p. 8 (Illustration) by Michael Caroleo; pp. 11 (Mars's surface), 12-13 (background), 14-15, 16-17 (Mars images), 19, 20-21 (panoramic view) courtesy of NASA/JPL/California Institute of Technology; pp. 12 (Olympus Mons) © CORBIS; 16 (view from Hawaii) © Gary Braasch/CORBIS; 20-21 (lander and rover) © Lowell Georgia/CORBIS.

Margaret, Amy.
  Mars/by Amy Margaret.—1st. ed.
    p. cm. — (the library of the planets.)
  Includes index.
  Summary: Describes the history, unique features, and exploration of Mars, the fourth planet from the Sun.
  ISBN 0-8239-5645-8 (lib. bdg.: alk. paper)
  1. Mars (Planet)–Juvenile literature. [1. Mars (Planet)] I. Title. II. Series.

QB641 .M33 2000
523.43–dc21   99-055186

Manufactured in the United States of America

Contents

If you weigh 100 lbs. (45.4 kg) on Earth, you will weigh 38 lbs. (17.2 kg) on Mars.

FUN FACTS

Mars, the Red Planet

Mars is the fourth planet from the Sun in our **solar system**. Our solar system is made up of the Sun, the nine planets, and their moons. Mars is over 140 million miles (225 million km) from the Sun. Our planet, Earth, is about 90 million miles (145 million km) away from the Sun. Mars is smaller than Earth. If Earth were hollow, you could fit seven planets the size of Mars inside it. Mars has a rocky surface with mountains, volcanoes, and canyons. If you look at it through a **telescope**, you can see its reddish color. This is why Mars is sometimes called the Red Planet.

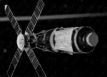

This drawing of the solar system was made by a computer. Mars is the third smallest planet in the solar system, after Pluto and Mercury.

Early Exploration of Mars

Mars is one of the planets closest to Earth. This made it easy for the world's first **astronomers** to spot it. In 1877, an astronomer named Giovanni Schiaparelli looked through his telescope. He thought he saw **canals** on Mars. He thought the canals carried water to cities on Mars. This would mean that there was life on the planet. A man named Percival Lowell studied astronomy and agreed with Schiaparelli about life on Mars. Lowell also thought that he saw canals when he looked at Mars through his telescope. Both men were wrong. The canals had actually been formed billions of years ago by running water. The water had long since dried up. There were no cities on Mars either. The idea of finding life on Mars did not end with Lowell, though. It still excites many people today.

Mars is named after the Roman god of war because of its blood-red color.

Sun

Mars

Planet	Orbit Time Around Sun
Mercury	88 Earth days
Venus	225 Earth days
Earth	365 Earth days
Mars	687 Earth days
Jupiter	12 Earth years
Saturn	29 Earth years
Uranus	84 Earth years
Neptune	165 Earth years
Pluto	248 Earth years

FUN FACTS

How Mars and the Planets Move

All nine planets in our solar system **orbit**, or circle, the Sun. It is the force of the Sun that pulls the planets around it. The closer a planet is to the Sun, the faster it travels around it. It takes Earth, the third planet from the Sun, 365 days to circle the Sun. That is why we say one year on Earth equals 365 days. Mars moves much more slowly. It takes Mars 687 Earth days, or nearly two years, to travel around the Sun.

Along with circling the Sun, each planet spins on its **axis**. The motion of a planet on its axis is like a merry-go-round. Both Mars and Earth make a complete turn on their axes in about 24 hours, which is equal to one full day.

It takes Mars nearly two years to travel around the Sun.

Comparing Mars and Earth

Both Mars and Earth have axes that tilt to the side. Other planets have axes that are straight up and down. The tilt on Mars and Earth causes the change in seasons. The seasons on Mars are summer and winter. They last about twice as long as summer and winter on Earth. Mars and Earth both have mountains, canyons, volcanoes, and rocky deserts. There are ice caps on the North and South poles of both planets. Earth's ice caps are made of water, and Mars's ice caps are made of frozen carbon dioxide. Carbon dioxide is the gas we **exhale**. It is poisonous to humans if breathed in. The biggest difference between the two planets is that so far no life has been found on Mars. A lot of Mars has still not been explored, however. Scientists continue to look for life or signs of past life on the planet.

These pictures of Earth (left) and Mars (right) were made by a computer. Below Earth is a photograph of a mountain range taken from space. Below Mars is a photograph of the surface of the planet.

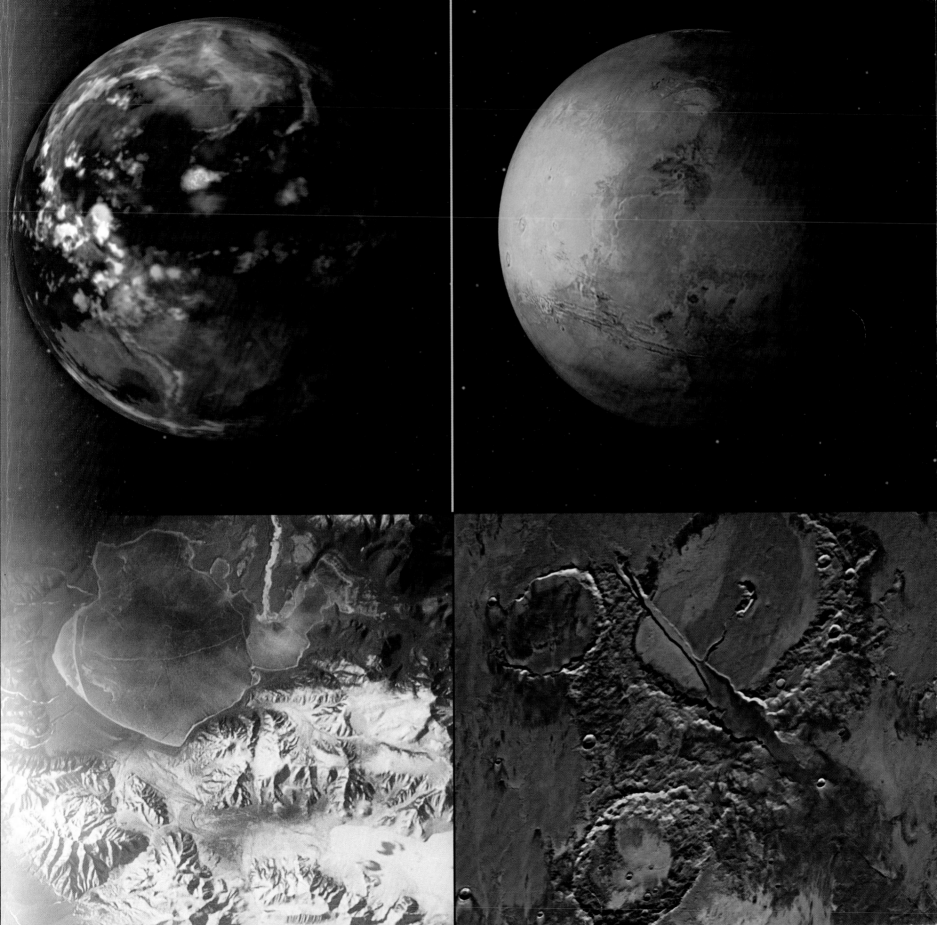

The Surface of Mars

Pictures of Mars show a surface of dry land covered in a layer of reddish brown dust. Iron is a metal found in the dust on Mars. Its red color makes the planet look red. There are rocks all over the planet, and there are no signs of running water. Scientists have clues that liquid water was once on Mars. One clue is a large, flat spot in the northern area of the planet. It looks like a dried-up sea floor.

There are four huge volcanoes on Mars called the Tharsis Montes. The tops of the Tharsis Montes are flat and go on for hundreds of miles (km). Long streams of **lava** flow out from the tops of these volcanoes. Olympus Mons is the largest known volcano in our solar system, reaching up to 75,000 feet (22,860 m) high. Its main **crater** is 40 miles (64.4 km) across. The tallest mountain on Earth, Mount Everest, is only 29,028 feet (8,848 m) high.

This image of the Olympus Mons was taken from space. The Olympus Mons is very large, about the size of the state of Texas (shown in outline around the picture).

The Moons of Mars

Phobos and Deimos are the two moons of Mars. They were both discovered in 1877 by American astronomer Asaph Hall. Hall named them Phobos and Deimos. Phobos and Deimos were the names of the **chariot** horses that belonged to the Roman god Mars. Earth has one moon that is 2,160 miles (3,476 km) across. The moons of Mars are much smaller. Phobos is about 17 miles (27.4 km) at its longest point, and Deimos is about 10 miles (16.1 km). The moons of Mars move quicker than Earth's Moon. Phobos speeds around Mars in a little over seven hours, and Deimos travels around Mars in a little over one Earth day. It takes Earth's Moon four weeks to move around the Earth. Both Phobos and Deimos

Deimos

Phobos

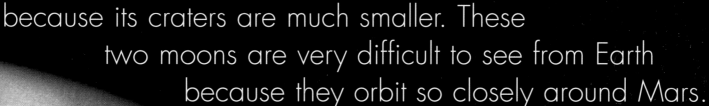

have dark surfaces, unlike Mars's reddish color. Both moons are covered in a thin layer of soil. The surface of Phobos is marked with many large craters. Deimos looks smoother because its craters are much smaller. These two moons are very difficult to see from Earth because they orbit so closely around Mars.

Mars's moon Phobos is shaped like a potato. It is 3,700 miles (6,000 km) away from Mars. Deimos, Mars's other moon, orbits 12,500 miles (20,000 km) above the planet.

Moon

Mars

Venus

KEEP A RECORD
One of the easiest ways to watch for changes on the surface of Mars is by drawing what you see. Begin with a small circle, then add lines, shading, and other details as you see them. Be sure to record the date and time. Keep this Mars record for several months to see what changes take place.

FUN FACTS

Seeing Mars From Earth

Mars is best seen through a telescope. You should be able to see a reddish color around the planet. You may be able to spot ice caps at the north and south ends, dark markings on the surface, or even a dust storm. If you know where to look, you might even find the planet without using a telescope or a pair of **binoculars**.

You will be able to see Mars at dawn from fall to the early spring. From spring to early summer, it is best to look for Mars in the evening sky. A monthly sky chart can help you figure out the best times to see Mars. For the latest on night sky planet sightings, check out the following Internet addresses. They will give you the most up-to-date information on when to see Mars.

http://www.kidsnspace.org/what_can_i_see.htm
http://www.skypub.com/sights/sights.shtml

The two views of Mars at the top of the page were taken by the Hubble Space Telescope. This telescope orbits Earth and sends images of the solar system to scientists on the ground. The labeled image of Mars was taken from the ground in the state of Hawaii.

In July 1965, *Mariner 4* was the first **space probe** to fly by Mars. It took pictures of its surface, which looked like the cratered surface of Earth's Moon. In the early 1970s, *Mariner 9* took pictures of Mars that showed proof of volcanoes and **channels** formed by running water. NASA (National Aeronautics Space Administration) sent the first spacecrafts to land on Mars in 1976. These crafts, called *Viking 1* and *Viking 2*, had heat sensors. A heat sensor is an instrument that measures how much heat an object gives off. Another type of sensor looked for objects giving off moisture. These missions also took dirt samples from the ground on Mars, tested them, and sent the results back to Earth through a computer. The tests showed that there was no life in the areas that were studied.

The two ball-shaped images of Mars show the planet's surface on its two hemispheres, or sides. The image at the top shows Mars's craters and the image at the far right, its volcanoes. The red line points out the height of different volcanoes.

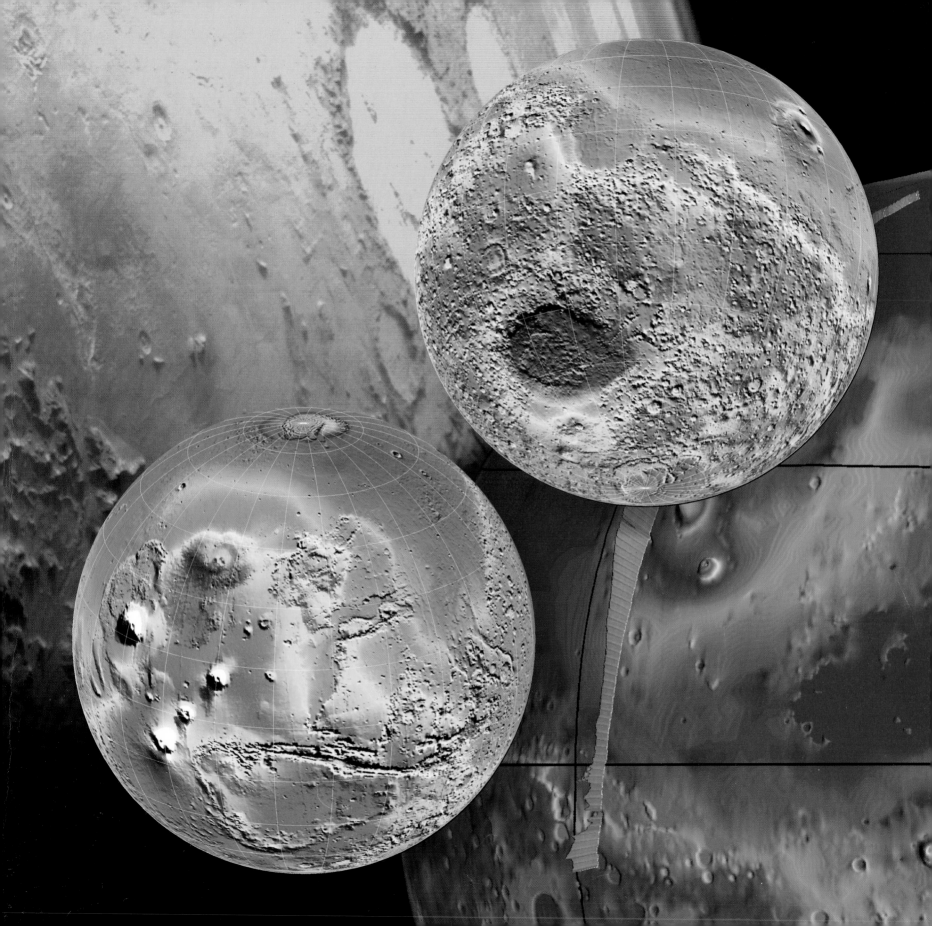

Landing On Mars

Twenty years after *Viking 1* and *Viking 2* landed on Mars, the *Mars Pathfinder* was **launched** in December 1996. It arrived on Mars on July 4, 1997.

The goal of the mission was to land a spacecraft safely on Mars. The *Mars Pathfinder* did land safely. It also tested rock samples. The *Pathfinder* had two parts, a **rover** and a **lander**. The rover was two feet (.61 m) long and one foot (.31 m) high. It took

For even more information and pictures of the *Mars Pathfinder* go to http://mars.jpl.nasa.gov/default.html

FUN FACTS

pictures and collected data as it rolled carefully along the soil of Mars. The lander sent back the photos and information to Earth through computers. The last time it sent something back was on September 27, 1997. Scientists on Earth tried to make contact with the lander several times after that. They were not able to connect with it. The mission was declared officially over in March 1998.

The Mars Pathfinder's lander (left) and rover (right) took pictures of the surface of Mars, as shown below.

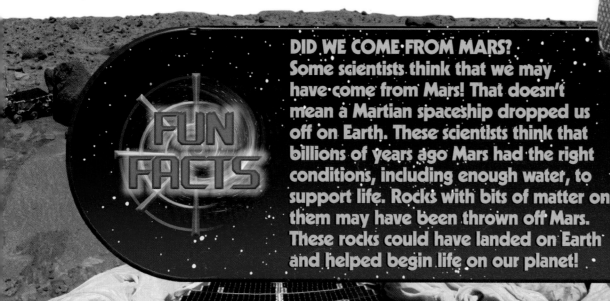

DID WE COME FROM MARS?
Some scientists think that we may have come from Mars! That doesn't mean a Martian spaceship dropped us off on Earth. These scientists think that billions of years ago Mars had the right conditions, including enough water, to support life. Rocks with bits of matter on them may have been thrown off Mars. These rocks could have landed on Earth and helped begin life on our planet!

FUN FACTS

Future Missions to Mars

Besides planet Earth, Mars is the most studied planet in our solar system. Not every mission to Mars has been a success, though. A spacecraft called the *Mars Lander* was due to set down on the planet in December of 1999. It was supposed to study the southern pole of Mars and look for ice and proof of water. However, scientists on Earth lost contact with the lander on December 3, just as it was heading into Mars's atmosphere. In February of 2000, scientists decided to stop trying to get a signal from the lander. Maybe we will hear from the lander in the future. One thing is for sure, though. With all the attention given to this neighbor of Earth, don't be surprised to see people landing on Mars in the next 10 to 20 years. Who knows? You might even be one of them!

Glossary

astronomers (ah-STRAH-nuh-merz) People who study the night sky, the planets, moons, stars, and other objects found there.

axis (AK-sis) A straight line on which an object turns or seems to turn.

binoculars (bih-NAH-kyuh-lurz) Hand-held lenses that make distant things appear closer.

canals (ka-NALZ) Bodies of water that are usually narrow.

channels (CHAN-ulz) The beds of a stream or river.

chariot (CHAR-ee-ot) A two-wheeled carriage pulled by horses.

crater (KRAY-ter) A hole in the ground that is shaped like a bowl.

exhale (eks-HAYL) To breathe out.

lander (LAN-der) A space vehicle designed to land on a planet.

launched (LAWNCHD) Pushed out or put into the air.

lava (LAH-vuh) A hot liquid made of melted rock that comes out of a volcano.

orbit (OR-bit) To circle around something.

rover (RO-ver) A vehicle used to explore the surface of a planet.

solar system (SOH-ler SIS-tem) A group of planets that circle a star. Our solar system has nine planets, which circle the Sun.

space probe (SPAYS PROHB) A spacecraft that travels in space and is steered by scientists on the ground.

telescope (TEL-uh-skohp) A tool that makes distant objects appear close up.

Index

A
astronomers, 6
axis, 9, 10

B
binoculars, 17

C
canals, 6
carbon dioxide, 10
crater, 13, 15, 18

H
Hall, Asaph, 14

L
Lowell, Percival, 6

M
Mariner 4, 18
Mariner 9, 18
Mars Lander, 22
Mars Pathfinder, 20–21
moons, 5, 14, 15, 18

O
Olympus Mons, 13

S
Schiaparelli, Giovanni, 6
solar system, 5, 9, 13, 22
space probe, 18

T
telescope, 5, 6, 17
Tharsis Montes, 13

V
Viking 1, 18, 20
Viking 2, 18, 20

Web Sites

If you would like to learn more about Mars check out these Web sites:
http://seds.lpl.arizona.edu/nineplanets/nineplanets/nineplanets.html
http://nssdc.gsfc.nasa.gov/planetary/planets/marspage.html
http://nssdc.gsfc.nasa.gov/planetary/chrono_future.html